I0428195

United States Government Accountability Office

Report to Congressional Requesters

September 2013

COMMUNITY POLICING HIRING GRANTS

Grant Application and Monitoring Processes Could Be Improved to Further Ensure Grantees Advance Community Policing

COMMUNITY POLICING HIRING GRANTS

Grant Application and Monitoring Processes Could Be Improved to Further Ensure Grantees Advance Community Policing

GAO Highlights

Highlights of GAO-13-521, a report to congressional requesters

Why GAO Did This Study

Since its 1994 inception, the U.S. Department of Justice's (DOJ) COPS Office has awarded roughly $14 billion in grants to support the advancement of community policing, which is a policing approach that proactively addresses the conditions that give rise to public safety issues, such as crime and social disorder. GAO was asked to review key grant management practices within the COPS Office. This report focuses on the largest of its programs—CHP, which awards grants to law enforcement agencies to hire law enforcement officers, rehire officers who have been laid off, or prevent scheduled officer layoffs. This report addresses: (1) From fiscal years 2008 through 2012, in what areas of the country was CHP funding disbursed and to what extent did award amounts vary during this period? (2) To what extent does the COPS Office's grant application collect information about how applicants plan to use CHP-funded officers to advance community policing? (3) To what extent does the COPS Office's monitoring process assess whether grantees are using funds to advance community policing?

GAO examined budget data and monitoring reports for 55 grantees, interviewed agency officials, and evaluated CHP applications from a systematic random sample of 103 CHP grants awarded from fiscal years 2010 through 2012.

What GAO Recommends

GAO recommends that the COPS Office revise and clarify the CHP application and enhance guidance to require monitors to document their analysis results of non-supplanting in monitoring reports. The COPS Office generally concurred with the recommendations and described actions to address them.

View GAO-13-521. For more information, contact David C. Maurer at (202) 512-9627 or maurerd@gao.gov.

What GAO Found

Nearly half of the Office of Community Oriented Policing Services (COPS) Hiring Program (CHP) funding from fiscal years 2008 through 2012 was awarded to grantees in six states, and award amounts varied considerably in certain years. During this period, state, county, and city law enforcement agencies nationwide received CHP grant awards to hire or rehire officers to advance community policing, with 48 percent of the funds awarded to grantees in California, Florida, Michigan, New Jersey, Ohio, and Texas. For grantees awarded the same number of officers, differences were driven mainly by variation across grantees' respective entry-level officer salaries and benefits. Variation in grantee award amounts were more prominent during 2009, 2010, and 2011, when salary and benefit levels were not statutorily capped, and grantees with higher officer salary and benefit levels generally received more CHP funding relative to other CHP grantees for the same number of officers.

The COPS Office's CHP application collects information required by statute from grant applicants, but could be further enhanced by revising the application to clarify for applicants that CHP-funded officers are required to be the personnel specifically engaged in the community policing activities described on the application. The application asks applicants to provide information on how they plan to implement community policing agency-wide, but does not specifically ask applicants to explain how CHP-funded officers will be deployed in community policing—the primary statutory purpose of the CHP program. According to GAO analysis of a systematic random sample of 103 CHP-funded applications, GAO estimated that less than 20 percent of the applications funded in 2010, 2011, and 2012 contained evidence showing how additional officers would be deployed in community policing. The Domestic Working Group's guide for grant accountability recommends that agencies require applicants to include information describing, among other things, their approach for using the funds and the specific activities that are crucial to the success of the program. Revising the application to clarify for applicants that CHP-funded officers are required to be the personnel specifically engaged in the community policing activities described on the application, consistent with best practices, would better position the COPS office to ascertain from applicants how these particular officers' activities would advance community policing.

The COPS Office's risk-based approach to monitoring assesses how grantees are using funds to advance community policing, but could be improved through additional monitoring guidance. The authorizing statute for the COPS grant programs contains a prohibition against supplanting— using federal funds to replace state or local funds. The COPS Office developed standards and an operations manual for monitors to use in assessing the potential for supplanting. For 5 of the 21 grantees at risk for supplanting, GAO found that the monitors did not document their analyses of supplanting and it was not clear how they reached conclusions regarding supplanting. The manual requires monitors to document their supplanting analysis in instances in which supplanting is identified, but does not have this requirement for non-supplanting. According to internal control standards, the documentation of agency activities is a key element of accountability for decisions. By enhancing the COPS Office's monitoring guidance to require monitors to document their results where the determination is made that supplanting has not occurred, the COPS Office may be better positioned to ensure that monitors are consistently assessing supplanting and that CHP funding is supplementing and not replacing state and local funding.

_____ United States Government Accountability Office

Contents

Figures

Abbreviations

CHP	COPS Hiring Program
CHRP	COPS Hiring Recovery Program
COPS	Office of Community Oriented Policing Services
CPD	Community Policing Development
CSPP	Child Sexual Predator Program
DOJ	Department of Justice
GAT	Grant Assessment Tool
ICAC	Internet Crimes Against Children
IG	Inspector General
OAAM	Office of Audit, Assessment, and Management
OJP	Office of Justice Programs
SOS	Secure Our Schools
TRGP	Tribal Resources Grant Program
UHP	Universal Hiring Program
VCCLEA	Violent Crime Control and Law Enforcement Act of 1994

This is a work of the U.S. government and is not subject to copyright protection in the
United States. The published product may be reproduced and distributed in its entirety
without further permission from GAO. However, because this work may contain
copyrighted images or other material, permission from the copyright holder may be
necessary if you wish to reproduce this material separately.

GAO
U.S. GOVERNMENT ACCOUNTABILITY OFFICE
441 G St. N.W.
Washington, DC 20548

September 25, 2013

The Honorable F. James Sensenbrenner, Jr.
Chairman
Subcommittee on Crime, Terrorism,
  Homeland Security, and Investigations
Committee on the Judiciary
House of Representatives

The Honorable Lamar Smith
House of Representatives

Since its 1994 inception, the U.S. Department of Justice's (DOJ) Office of Community Oriented Policing Services (COPS)—known as the COPS Office—has awarded roughly $14 billion in grants to law enforcement agencies to support the advancement of community policing, which is a policing approach that proactively addresses, through law-enforcement-community engagement, the conditions that give rise to public safety issues, such as crime, social disorder, and fear of crime.[1] Though the focus of grant funding over time has varied, COPS Office funding has supported, among other things, police officer hiring, drug education programs, and law enforcement technologies to advance community policing. From 1995 through 2002, the average annual COPS appropriation was more than $1 billion.[2] Beginning in fiscal year 2003, annual appropriations for the program, in general, started to decrease. The average annual appropriation for the COPS program from 2003-2012 (excluding the $1 billion in funding COPS received under the American

---

[1]Prior to the 1994 establishment of the COPS Office, in December 1993, DOJ's Bureau of Justice Assistance awarded community policing grants to hire officers under the Police Hiring Supplement Program, which was established by the Supplemental Appropriations Act of 1993, Pub. L. No.103-50, 107 Stat. 241, 246 (1993). In this report, when we refer to COPS Office funding dating back to 1993, we are including this program.

[2]The year 1995 was the first in which the COPS Office administered funds appropriated for community policing.

Recovery and Reinvestment Act of 2009[3]) was approximately $596 million.[4]

In recent years, Members of Congress expressed interest in improving oversight and accountability of federal grant programs; for example, the House Committee on the Judiciary held a hearing on oversight of the COPS Office in 2012.[5] During the 2012 hearing, a Member of Congress noted concerns about the extent to which COPS grants had been used for purposes consistent with program goals and whether or not supplanting—using federal funds to replace state or local funds—had occurred. Our prior work on DOJ grants has identified opportunities to improve DOJ grants administration. Specifically, in our prior review of overlap among DOJ grant programs, we recommended that the Attorney General, among other things, assess DOJ grant programs, including the COPS grant program, for potential overlap and harmonize departmental business processes for grants management.[6] Our past work on grants management across the federal government has found that opportunities exist to improve the design and implementation of federal grants: in particular, data collection and validation.[7] Additionally, for the past 10 years, the DOJ Office of Inspector General (IG) has identified grant

---

[3]Pub. L. No. 111-5, 123 Stat. 115, 130.

[4] For fiscal year 2013, the appropriation for the COPS Program is $209.7 million, after taking into account the reduction to all nonexempt appropriations accounts based on the March 1, 2013, sequestration.

[5] Hearing on the U.S. Department of Justice Community Oriented Policing Services Office" February 29, 2012 (Serial No. 112-97).

[6]GAO, *Justice Grant Programs: DOJ Should Do More to Reduce the Risk of Unnecessary Duplication and Enhance Program Assessment*, GAO-12-517 (Washington, D.C: July 12, 2012). We made eight recommendations to ensure that DOJ can identify overlapping grant programs to either consolidate or coordinate similar programs, mitigate the risk of unnecessary grant award duplication in its programs, and enhance DOJ's ability to gauge grant program effectiveness. DOJ has taken steps to partially address these recommendations, although they still remain open.

[7]GAO, *Grants Performance: Justice and FEMA Collect Performance Data for Selected Grants, but Action Needed to Validate FEMA Performance Data*, GAO-13-552 (Washington, D.C.: June 24, 2013); *Grants to State and Local Governments: An Overview of Federal Funding Levels and Selected Challenges*, GAO-12-1016 (Washington, D.C.: Sept. 25, 2012), and *Grants Management: Enhancing Performance Accountability Provisions Could Lead to Better Results*, GAO-06-1046 (Washington, D.C.: Sept. 29, 2006).

management among its list of top management challenges.[8] The level of federal spending on grant programs combined with the federal government's continued long-term fiscal challenges and constrained budget underscores the importance of ensuring that agencies employ sound grants management practices.

You requested that we review the COPS Office funding trends and the office's overall grant management and oversight practices of its community policing grants. The COPS Hiring Program (CHP) and its predecessors, the Universal Hiring Program (UHP) and the COPS Hiring Recovery Program (CHRP)—in this report referred to collectively as CHP—account for 68 percent of the funds that the COPS Office has awarded through its various grant programs from fiscal years 2008 through 2012.[9] This report focuses on the CHP program, and answers the following questions: (1) From fiscal years 2008 through 2012, in what areas of the country was CHP funding disbursed and to what extent did award amounts vary during this period? (2) To what extent does the COPS Office's grant application collect information about how applicants plan to use CHP-funded officers to advance community policing? (3) To what extent does the COPS Office's monitoring process assess whether grantees are using funds to advance community policing?

To address the first question, we reviewed the history of the COPS Office's programs and related award data from the most recent 5 fiscal years—2008 through 2012—and confirmed that CHP received the largest share of funds as compared with other programs administered by the COPS Office during this period. We also analyzed COPS Office documentation, such as the *Grant Owner's Manuals* and COPS Office website materials, to learn about each program's origin and emphasis. To determine which areas of the United States have received CHP funding, we analyzed the allocation of CHP grant awards—and the numbers of

---

[8]Additionally, the DOJ OIG issued a report in 2009 on the COPS Office which identified six steps intended to improve the office's awarding and monitoring of grants. DOJ Office of the Inspector General, *Improving the Office of Community Oriented Policing Services' Grant Awarding, Monitoring, and Program Evaluation Processes,* (Washington D.C.: June, 2009).

[9]UHP grants were awarded in 2008, and COPS Hiring Recovery Program grants were awarded in 2009; both grant programs, l ke CHP, sought to advance community policing by supporting the hiring or rehiring of officers or helping grantees to avoid scheduled officer layoffs.

officers funded—by state and mapped the CHP grant award data. Additionally, we analyzed CHP award lists for fiscal years 2008 through 2012 to determine the average CHP entry-level officer salary and benefits by state and territory, and assessed them for variation.[10] To ensure the reliability of data used in our review, we interviewed COPS Office officials about the integrity of the data they provided to us and reviewed system tests that the COPS Office conducts periodically to ensure data reliability. We determined that the data were sufficiently reliable for the purposes of our report. We also interviewed COPS Office officials to determine what factors could account for variations in grant award amounts and to learn about other administrative aspects of the program.

To address the second question, we examined the CHP authorizing statute, the CHP application, and the COPS Office's criteria for selecting awardees. We compared the CHP application with the CHP authorizing statute and best practices for grants management, including practices for designing applications, identified by the Domestic Working Group.[11] Additionally, we selected a systematic random sample of 103 CHP applications, out of 841, that the COPS Office funded from the 3 most recent fiscal years—2010 through 2012—and reviewed them for their level of detail in describing applicants' planned use of funds.[12] The results of this review are generalizable to all 841 funded applications.[13] Further,

---

[10]In our review of grant award lists from fiscal years 2008 through 2012, we reviewed the years 2009 through 2011 together as one group, because during this period awards were not subject to statutory salary and benefit caps; thus the COPS Office awarded each grantee the full amount it cost the grantee to pay the salaries and benefits of each funded officer. We reviewed 2008 and 2012 individually because in both fiscal years 2008 and 2012, salary caps were in place, as we discuss later in the report.

[11]Domestic Working Group, Grant Accountability Project, *Guide to Opportunities for Improving Grant Accountability* (Washington, D.C.: October 2005). The Domestic Working Group first convened in 2005 to provide a forum for audit organizations to identify ways to improve grant accountability. It is composed of federal government inspectors general and other state and local audit organizations, and is chaired by the Comptroller General of the United States.

[12]A systematic random sample is a method of sample selection in which the population is listed in some order, in this instance dollar amount of grant awarded, and every kth element is selected randomly for the sample. We selected 2010 through 2012 because they reflected the most recent active CHP awards, each of which remains open for a 3-year grant term.

[13]With the finite population correction factor, the precision for estimates drawn from this sample is no greater than plus or minus 9 percentage points at the 95 percent level of confidence.

we conducted interviews with a nonprobability sample of 20 CHP grantees in five metropolitan areas to understand how they were using their awards at the local level. We selected these grantees based on the amount of the CHP award each grantee received, geographical variation, and the population size served by the grantee. The results of these interviews were not generalizable, but provided illustrative examples of the activities in which grantees engaged with their CHP funds. Finally, we interviewed COPS Office officials who oversee the application process to gather further information on the design of the application, including how the applications were scored.

To address the third question, we obtained and examined the monitoring reports for 55 grantees awarded CHP grants from the 3 most recent fiscal years: 2010 through 2012.[14] The COPS Office produces these reports following the on-site monitoring visits it conducts with grantees to assess their progress and identify compliance issues, such as supplanting, for CHP grants. We then compared these monitoring reports with COPS Office guidance, such as its grant-monitoring standards, as well as with Standards for Internal Control in the Federal Government and best practices for grant program management from the Domestic Working Group, to evaluate the extent to which the monitors assessed whether grantees had used grant funds to supplant local funds.[15] Additionally, we discussed the COPS Office's grant-monitoring practices with officials from DOJ's Office of Audit, Assessment, and Management (OAAM) to discuss

---

[14]As with the grant applications we selected for review, we selected these 3 years because they reflected the most recent active CHP awards, each of which remains open for a 3-year grant term. These 55 grantees were all of the grantees from this period for which the COPS Office had completed CHP grant-monitoring reports at the time we began our audit. As discussed later in the report, these grantees are selected using risk-based monitoring criteria.

[15]GAO, Standards for Internal Control in the Federal Government, GAO/AIMD 00-21.3.1 (Washington, D.C.: November 1999); COPS Office, Grant Monitoring Standards and Guidelines for Hiring and Redeployment (Washington D.C.: Sept. 16, 2004) and Grant Monitoring Division Monitoring Operations Manual: Administrative and Compliance (Washington D.C.: May 4, 2010); Domestic Working Group, Grant Accountability Project, Guide to Opportunities for Improving Grant Accountability (Washington, D.C.: October 2005).

GAO-13-521 Community Policing Hiring Grants

its role in oversight of monitoring activities at the COPS Office.[16] We also interviewed COPS Office officials who oversee the monitoring process about their monitoring practices, and the extent to which on-site reviews enable them to identify and document instances of potential supplanting. Finally, we obtained the perspective of the COPS Office on the performance of its grant monitors in assessing and documenting instances of potential supplanting identified during our review of monitoring reports. Appendix I contains further information on our scope and methodology.

We conducted this performance audit from August 2012 to September 2013 in accordance with generally accepted government auditing standards. Those standards require that we plan and perform the audit to obtain sufficient, appropriate evidence to provide a reasonable basis for our findings and conclusions based on our audit objectives. We believe that the evidence obtained provides a reasonable basis for our findings and conclusions based on our audit objectives.

Background

Community Policing

The Public Safety Partnership and Community Policing Act of 1994, as amended, authorizes grants to states, units of local government, Indian tribal governments, other public and private entities, and multi-jurisdictional or regional consortia for a variety of community policing-related purposes.[17] Among other things, this includes the hiring and rehiring of law enforcement officers for deployment in community policing and developing and implementing innovative programs to permit members of the community to assist law enforcement agencies in the prevention of crime in the community. The act also requires that grantees not supplant state and local funding, but rather use the federal funds for

---

[16]OAAM works to improve and enhance programmatic oversight for the Office of Justice Programs (OJP), as well as the COPS Office and the Office on Violence Against Women. OAAM has four main responsibilities: (1) ensure financial grant compliance and auditing of OJP's internal controls to prevent waste, fraud, and abuse; (2) conduct program assessments of OJP and COPS Office grant programs; (3) oversee monitoring activities; and (4) serve as a central source for grant management policy.

[17]Enacted as Title I of the Violent Crime Control and Law Enforcement Act of 1994, Pub. L. No. 103-322, 108 Stat. 1796 (codified as amended at 42 U.S.C. §§ 3796dd – dd-8).

activities beyond what would have been available without a grant.[18] To administer the grant funds authorized by the act, the Attorney General created the COPS Office in October 1994. Since 1994, the COPS Office has awarded roughly $14 billion to advance community policing through its various grant programs.

The COPS Office defines community policing in its CHP applications and *Grant Owner's Manual*, issued annually, as "a philosophy that promotes organizational strategies, which support the systematic use of partnerships and problem-solving techniques, to proactively address the immediate conditions that give rise to public safety issues, such as crime, social disorder, and fear of crime."[19] The CHP grant applications describe some of these terms:

- **community partnerships**: collaborative partnerships between the law enforcement agency and the individuals and organizations they serve to both develop solutions to problems and increase trust in police;
- **organizational transformation**: the alignment of organizational management, structure, personnel and information systems to support community partnerships and proactive problem-solving efforts; and
- **problem solving:** the process of engaging in the proactive and systematic examination of identified problems to develop effective responses that are rigorously evaluated.

A characteristic of community policing is its emphasis on proactive policing—an approach to preventing crime—which is contrasted with traditional, reactive policing—an approach that responds to crime—both of which the interactive figure 1 illustrates.

---

[18]42 U.S.C. § 3796dd-3. For the purpose of COPS Office grants, supplanting means using COPS Office grant funds to replace state or local funding—or, in the case of Indian tribal governments, funding supplied by the Bureau of Indian Affairs—that otherwise would have been spent on the specific law enforcement purpose of the COPS Office grant award.

[19]Developed by the COPS Office to ensure that all CHP grantees clearly understand and meet the requirements of the grant, the CHP *Grant Owner's Manual* assists agencies with the administrative and financial matters associated with the CHP grant.

GAO-13-521 Community Policing Hiring Grants

Move the mouse over the icons to view more information. This additional information is also reproduced in appendix II for readers of printed copies.

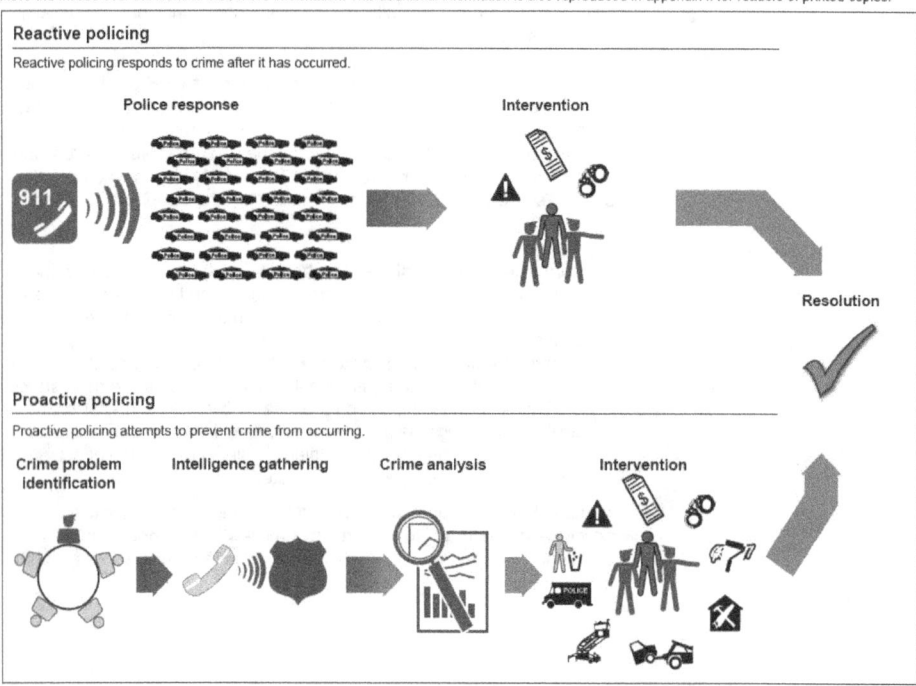

Source: GAO.

From fiscal years 2008 through 2012, the COPS Office managed 10 programs designed to advance community policing. As table 1 illustrates, these 10 programs provided funding to target crime issues, such as school violence, as well as to hire officers or develop crime-fighting technology, among other things.

Table 1: Grant Programs Managed by the COPS Office from Fiscal Years 2008 through 2012

Program	Description and fiscal years grants were awarded	Amount funded	Percentage of total funds
COPS Hiring Program (CHP), COPS Hiring Recovery Program (CHRP), and COPS Universal Hiring Program (UHP)	Available to law enforcement agencies to hire law enforcement officers, re-hire law enforcement officers who have been laid off, or prevent scheduled law enforcement officer layoffs in order to advance community policing. The funded law enforcement officers must be engaged in community policing, or an equal number of the grantee's veteran law enforcement officers must be redeployed to community policing. Awarded in fiscal years 2008-2012.[a]	$1,681,555,221	68
Technology programs	Available to non-federal law enforcement agencies to develop technologies to advance community policing and help fight crime. Awarded in fiscal years 2008-2010.	$533,638,587	21
Tribal Resources Grant Program	Available to support implementation or enhancement of community policing efforts by tribal law enforcement agencies to implement or enhance community policing efforts. Designed to increase collaboration between law enforcement agencies and members of the community by providing a variety of funding options including officer background investigations, basic and specialized law enforcement training, uniforms, standard issue equipment, department-wide technology, and police vehicles. Awarded in fiscal years 2008-2012.	$133,809,157	5
Secure Our Schools	Available to non-federal law enforcement agencies and schools to work collaboratively to purchase crime prevention equipment and to provide safety training to staff and students to improve security and prevent violence at schools and on school grounds. Awarded in fiscal years 2008-2011.	$59,493,666	2
Child Sexual Predator Program	Available to nonfederal law enforcement agencies that district U.S. Attorney's Offices or the U.S. Marshals Service nominated to establish or enhance strategies to locate, arrest, and prosecute child sexual predators and exploiters through support for such efforts as Internet Crimes Against Children (ICAC) task forces, as well as enforce state sex offender registration laws. ICAC is a network of 61 task forces composed of federal, state, local, and tribal law enforcement and prosecutorial agencies that engage in investigations, forensic examinations, and prosecutions of Internet crimes against children. Awarded in fiscal years 2008-2011.	$40,885,133	2

Program	Description and fiscal years grants were awarded	Amount funded	Percentage of total funds
Community Policing Development	Available to public governmental agencies, profit and non-profit institutions, universities, community groups, and faith-based organizations to advance the practice of community policing through training and technical assistance, the development of innovative community policing strategies, applied research, guidebooks, and best practices. Awarded in fiscal years 2008-2012.	$27,508,645	1
Tribal Methamphetamine Enforcement Program	Available to tribal law enforcement agencies to support their participation in the development of comprehensive strategies to combat methamphetamine production, use, and trafficking in tribal communities. Awarded in fiscal years 2010-2011.	$7,720,838	Less than 1
Safe Schools Initiative	Available to state and local agencies to assist in delinquency prevention, community planning and development, school safety resources, and technology development. Awarded in fiscal years 2008-2010.	$9,487,963	Less than 1
Total		$2,494,099,210	Less than 100[b]

Source: GAO analysis of COPS Office documents and award information.

[a] These grants were awarded under the UHP program in fiscal year 2008; the CHRP program in fiscal year 2009; and the CHP program in fiscal years 2010, 2011, and 2012.

[b] Percentages do not sum to 100 because of rounding.

COPS Hiring Program

As table 1 indicates, CHP accounted for 68 percent of the funds awarded through the COPS Office's various grant programs. The program provides these funds over a 3-year term, on a reimbursable basis, meaning that the COPS Office approves grants for a specified number of officer hires or rehires—in cases where officers have previously been laid off—but provides the funding to the law enforcement agencies once these officers are onboard. Grantees must use the funds to hire or rehire additional officers for deployment in community policing or can redeploy a commensurate number of experienced locally funded officers to community policing after the entry-level officers are hired with CHP funds. By law, each year CHP funding must be split in such a way that the total grant funding awarded to each eligible state—meaning the sum of the grants awarded to applicants in that state—equals at least one-half of 1 percent of the total CHP funding appropriated by Congress for that year.[20] At the same time, the law requires that CHP funding be evenly split between entities serving jurisdictions with populations exceeding 150,000 people and those serving jurisdictions with populations of 150,000 or

---

[20]42 U.S.C. §3796dd(f).

fewer.[21] Specific award provisions, such as salary and benefit caps per officer funded; grantee fund-matching requirements; and other nuances, including a recent emphasis on the hiring of veterans, have varied each year since the CHP's first authorization, in 1994. For example, in 2008 and 2012, pursuant to the statutory requirements for the grant program, grantees were required to match the CHP award with at least 25 percent of local nonfederal funds and salary caps of $75,000 and $125,000, respectively, applied. However, under the American Recovery and Reinvestment Act (Recovery Act) these requirements did not apply in 2009, 2010, and 2011.[22] Table 2 highlights changes in the CHP during the past 5 fiscal years that affected the amount of funding available to applicants as well as which applicants received funding.

Table 2: Annual Changes in Specific COPS Hiring Program (CHP) Award Provisions from Fiscal Years 2008 through 2012

Year	Statutory salary and benefits cap (per officer, spread over the 3-year grant period)	Other provisions
2008	Up to 75 percent of the approved entry-level salary and benefits (and thus a 25 percent local share) and a maximum federal share of $75,000 per officer position over 3 years.	Emphasized violent crime task force participation.
2009	Officer salary and benefits were not capped; no local share was required.	None.
2010	Officer salary and benefits were not capped; no local share was required.	Required that the number of officers an applicant requested could not exceed 5 percent of the law enforcement agency's sworn force for a maximum of 50 officers. For agencies with a sworn force of fewer than 20 officers, awards were limited to 1 officer. CHP grantees were selected from the pool of 2009 COPS Hiring Recovery Program (CHRP) applications submitted in the prior year that were not funded, or received partial funding of their capped request.
2011	Officer salary and benefits were not capped; no local share was required.	Required that the number of officers requested could not exceed 5 percent of agency's sworn force for a maximum of 25 officers. For agencies with a sworn force of less than 20 officers, awards were limited to 1 officer.

[21] 42 U.S.C. §§ 3793(a)(11)(B), 3796dd(h). In addition, an appropriate amount of available funds is to be made available for grants to Indian tribal governments or tribal law enforcement agencies.

[22] Two of the primary purposes of the Recovery Act were to "preserve and create jobs and promote economic recovery" and "stabilize State and local government budgets, in order to minimize and avoid reductions in essential services and counterproductive State and local tax increases." Pub. L. No. 111-5, § 3, 123 Stat. 115, 115-16.

GAO-13-521 Community Policing Hiring Grants

Year	Statutory salary and benefits cap (per officer, spread over the 3-year grant period)	Other provisions
2012	Up to 75 percent of the approved entry-level salary and benefits (and thus a 25 percent local share) and a maximum federal share of $125,000 per officer position over 3 years.	Emphasized hiring veterans. Agencies whose requests were fully funded in fiscal year 2011, or that received 25 officer positions, were not eligible to apply. CHP grantees were selected from the pool of 2011 applications submitted in the prior year that were not funded, or received partial funding of their capped request.

Source: GAO analysis of COPS Office documents and COPS authorizing statute and appropriations.

To select grantees for CHP, the COPS Office requires applicants to respond electronically to closed-end questions and provide a narrative description of the crime problems they are facing, among other things, in their grant applications. For example, one of the close-ended questions asks applicants to add a check mark if their agencies' strategic plans include specific goals or objectives relating to community partnerships or problem solving. Another close-ended question provides response categories for applicants to select the ways in which their agencies share information with community members. According to COPS Office officials, in consultation with the Associate Attorney General and the Deputy Attorney General, they establish weights for (1) community policing questions, (2) questions pertaining to the applicants' fiscal health, and (3) reported crime levels. They then score the applications and award funds to those applicants with the highest scores. For example, in fiscal years 2009 and 2010, fiscal health accounted for 50 percent, crime rates accounted for 35 percent, and community policing activities accounted for 15 percent of the total score.[23]

To monitor grantee performance, the COPS Office requires, as a term and condition of its grants, that grantees participate in grant-monitoring and -auditing activities, which can include programmatic and financial reviews of their funded activities. Accordingly, COPS Office officials stated that all grantees are required to submit quarterly progress reports that provide financial and programmatic information, such as their progress in implementing the community policing plan they described in their grant applications for utilizing CHP funds to advance community policing. According to the COPS Office, the goal of its monitoring is to assess grantees' stewardship of federal funding, performance, innovation, and community policing best practices resulting from COPS Office

---

[23]In fiscal year 2011, fiscal health accounted for 20 percent, crime rates accounted for 30 percent, and community policing activities accounted for 50 percent of the total score. The COPS scoring process varies from year to year.

funding. In addition, according to the COPS Office, because of the number of COPS Office grantees, the COPS Office selects a limited number of grants to monitor based upon a grantee's level of risk.[24] In addition to the size of the grant award, such risk factors include, but are not limited to, whether or not the grantee

- has prior federal grant experience,
- has submitted late reports of its progress or failed to submit progress reports entirely, and
- has requested grant extensions.

Nearly Half of CHP Funding In the Past 5 Years Was Awarded to Grantees in Six States, and Award Amounts Varied Considerably in Certain Years

As the interactive map in figure 2 illustrates, CHP grant awards were distributed throughout the United States from fiscal years 2008 through 2012.

---

[24]From 2010 through 2012, the COPS Office awarded 841 CHP grants, of which 55 were selected for on-site monitoring.

The interactive map can be accessed here:
http://www.gao.gov/products/GAO-13-521

Figure 2: Geographic Dispersion of COPS Hiring Program (CHP) Grant Awards, Number of Officers Funded, and CHP Compensation, Fiscal Years 2008 through 2012 (Interactive Graphic)

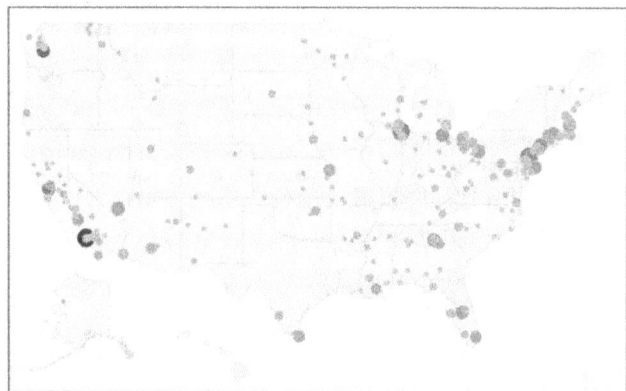

Source: GAO analysis of Department of Justice's Office of Community Oriented Policing Services (COPS) data

As figure 3 illustrates, 48 percent of the funding was awarded to grantees in six states—California, Florida, Michigan, New Jersey, Ohio, and Texas. Across all the states, grantees in California received the highest level of total CHP funding from 2008 through 2012. Specifically, total CHP awards in California equaled approximately $360 million, or more than 20 percent of the total CHP funding awarded.

Figure 3: Total COPS Hiring Program Funding by State from Fiscal Years 2008 through 2012

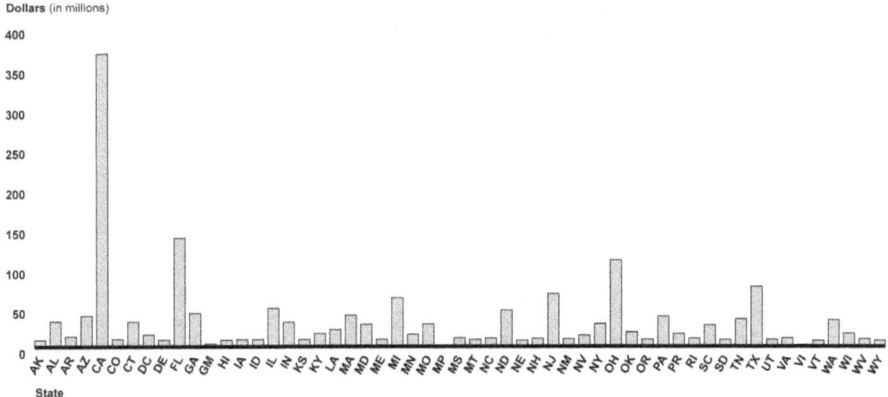

Dollars (in millions)

State

Source: GAO analysis of COPS Office grants awards and funding.

Note: Territories displayed include: Guam (GM), the Northern Mariana Islands (MP), Puerto Rico (PR), and the U.S. Virgin Islands (VI).

Officials from the COPS Office cited several factors that influenced the allocation of grant funds across the states and territories. In particular, officials pointed to the population-based statutory provision described previously, which requires the COPS Office to allocate 50 percent of available grant funding to jurisdictions with populations exceeding 150,000 and 50 percent to jurisdictions with a population of 150,000 or fewer. Officials noted that some states—for example, California—have more cities with populations exceeding 150,000 compared with other states. This enables a smaller number of states to compete for half of the total grant funding, while a greater number of states without cities of this size compete for the remaining half of the total. Further, these large cities tend to receive larger awards because they deploy comparatively more officers than smaller cities. Apart from a separate statutory provision, also described previously, which requires that each state receive at least one-half of 1 percent of the total CHP funding appropriated by Congress each year, COPS Office officials emphasized that a grantee's particular location is not prioritized over the application categories of community policing, crime data, and fiscal health. Regarding fiscal health, officials noted that certain states have been disproportionately affected by fiscal

GAO-13-521 Community Policing Hiring Grants

distress, a factor that is directly reflected in the fiscal health component of the CHP application. Finally, the number of law enforcement agencies—and thus potential applicants—varies across states, which contributes additional variation in how funding is ultimately distributed.

For grantees awarded the same number of officers, differences were driven mainly by variation across grantees' respective entry-level officer salaries and benefits—the only costs CHP allows. However, this variation was more prominent during years when salary and benefit levels were not statutorily capped: 2009 through 2011.[25] Thus, during the period 2009 through 2011, grantees with higher officer salary and benefit levels generally received more CHP funding relative to other CHP grantees to hire, rehire, or prevent layoffs for the same number of officers. For example, in fiscal year 2011, a grantee in California received a CHP award equivalent to its entry-level officer salary and benefits level of $150,753 per officer. In the same fiscal year, a grantee in Connecticut received a CHP award—also based on its entry-level officer salary and benefits—of $64,459 per officer per year. As a result of these local variations in per officer cost, this particular Connecticut grantee received and used 57 percent less federal funding to support each officer it hired or rehired compared with its California counterpart in this example. According to COPS Office officials, geographical differences in the cost of living could partly contribute to wage differences. Additionally, the availability of state and local budgetary resources to support law enforcement salaries and benefits may have affected wages. Further, COPS Office officials stated that other factors unique to certain areas of the country could account for the wage disparity that drives CHP costs. For example, some agencies may participate in more expensive state retirement systems or may not be able to set wages that align with market conditions because of union labor contract obligations. Figure 4 displays the average annual CHP-funded officer salary and benefit levels, by state and territory, for awards made from fiscal year 2009 through 2011—the years in which CHP grants awards were not capped.

---

[25]Pursuant to statutory authorization for CHP, awards are generally capped at $75,000; in 2008, this cap applied. In 2009, the Recovery Act eliminated the cap for fiscal years 2009 and 2010. This also applied to 2011 funds, because DOJ was operating under a continuing resolution, which provides budget authority for federal agencies to continue to fund their operations at a level consistent with previous year funding in the absence of annual appropriations. In 2012, appropriations language established a $125,000 cap.

Figure 4: Average Annual COPS Hiring Program (CHP)-Funded Officer Salary and Benefits among CHP Grantees, by State and Territory, from Fiscal Years 2009 through 2011

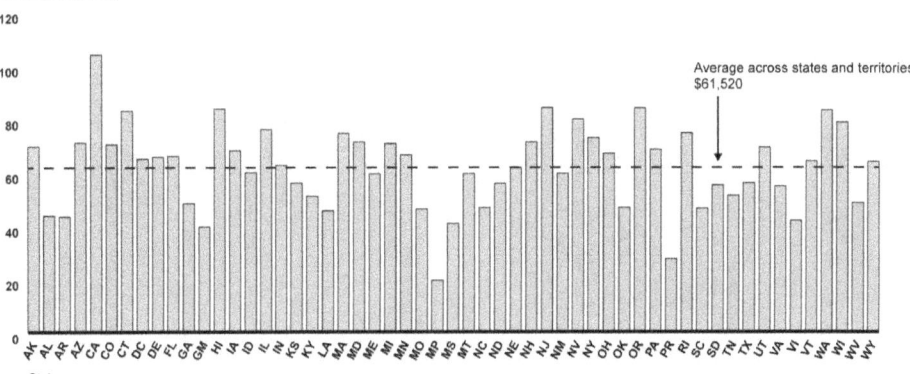

Dollars (in thousands)

Average across states and territories $61,520

State

Source: GAO analysis of COPS Office grants awards and funding.

Note: Territories displayed include Guam (GM), the Northern Mariana Islands (MP), Puerto Rico (PR), and the U.S. Virgin Islands (VI).

In contrast, statutory salary and benefit caps were in place for fiscal years 2008 and 2012; thus during these years, each grantee was limited to receiving the same per officer maximum, irrespective of local differences in salary and benefit levels. Any officer-related expenses over and above the cap were the independent funding responsibility of the grantee and were not covered by CHP funding. As a result, less variation in award amounts occurred in fiscal years 2008 and 2012—when there was a cap—as compared with fiscal years 2009, 2010, and 2011—when there was no cap. According to DOJ officials, some additional variation in average award amounts occurred in 2012 as a result of the COPS Office exercising statutory authority allowing the COPS Office Director to waive the $125,000 salary and benefit cap, as well as the matching requirement when awarding grants.[26] In 2012, the COPS Office granted 41 local match-and-cap waivers out of the 248 applicants that had requested them.[27]

Our analysis shows that interest in CHP funding remains high with the $125,000 per officer cap. From fiscal years 2008 through 2012, the COPS Office received more requests for CHP funding in grant applications than it could accommodate. The cap for fiscal year 2013 is $125,000, and in the President's budget request for fiscal year 2014, the cap remains at $125,000.

---

[26]42 U.S.C. §§ 3796dd(g), 3796dd-3(c); Consolidated and Further Continuing Appropriations Act, Pub. L. No. 112-55, div. B, 125 Stat. 618-19. The COPS Office Director may waive the requirement of both the officer funding cap for the hiring program and the minimum 25 percent local matching requirement for grantees. According to COPS Office officials, the COPS Office Director grants waivers for applicants that show the highest demonstrated need for financial assistance based upon the scored financial health section of the CHP grant application.

[27]CHP grantees in California received a majority of the waivers of the $125,000 salary and benefit award caps for fiscal year 2012.

The COPS Office's CHP Application Collects Information Required by Statute, but Could Be Further Enhanced by Clarifying that CHP-Funded Officers Are Required to Be Engaged in Community Policing Activities

The CHP application solicits information from applicants in accordance with statute, but the COPS office may realize benefits by revising the application to clarify for applicants that CHP-funded officers are required to be the personnel specifically engaged in the community policing activities described on the application.[28] The statute authorizing COPS Office grant programs requires applications, including the CHP application, to gather information from applicants related to several items, including, but not limited to the applicant's

- explanation of how the grant will be used to reorient its mission toward community policing or enhance its involvement in or commitment to community policing,
- specific public safety needs,
- inability to address the needs without federal assistance,
- plans for obtaining support at the conclusion of federal funding, and
- detailed implementation plan and long-term strategy that reflects consultation with community groups and appropriate private and public agencies.[29]

The statute does not further specify the content of these items, particularly the content of the detailed implementation plan and long-term strategy. However, the 2012 CHP application requires applicants to provide related information, such as how applicants plan to reorient their mission toward or enhance their involvement in or commitment to community policing. Specifically, COPS Office officials reported that the Law Enforcement & Community Policing Strategy section of the application is intended to obtain information from applicants to address the requirements of a detailed implementation plan and long-term strategy. For instance, this section requires applicants to include information on the crime problem that will be addressed with grant funds, information sources that will be used to improve the understanding of the problem and determine whether the response was effective, and the partnerships the agency will form.

---

[28]Since grantees can, after hiring entry-level officers with CHP funds, redeploy a commensurate number of experienced locally funded officers to community policing to satisfy the requirements of the grant, we are also referring to the activities of experienced locally funded officers deployed in support of community policing when we discuss the activities of CHP-funded officers.

[29]42 U.S.C. § 3796dd-1.

The application further requires applicants to indicate the community policing activities their entire agency was currently engaged in as well as those activities their organization intended to enhance or initiate with CHP funds. The fiscal year 2012 application notes that the COPS Office recognizes that CHP-funded officers will engage in a variety of community policing activities and strategies, including participating in some or all aspects of the applicant's implementation plan. However, the application does not specifically ask applicants to explain how CHP-funded officers will be deployed in community policing—the primary purpose of the CHP program as expressed by the statute.[30] For instance, the application does not ask applicants to provide information on what community policing activities, such as attending community meetings, CHP-funded officers will be undertaking.

The Domestic Working Group's guide for improving grant accountability provides best practices for designing grant applications, including specific elements that are recommended to be addressed in grant applications.[31] The Domestic Working Group, composed of federal government inspectors general and chaired by the Comptroller General of the United States, created the guide to share useful and innovative grant management approaches with government executives at the federal, state, and local levels.[32] Specifically, the Domestic Working Group's guide recommends that agencies require applicants to

- submit a detailed narrative as evidence of proper work planning to obtain and evaluate information from applicants when making award decisions, and
- include information to link grant activities with results, which is often referred to as logic modeling. As part of the logic model approach, applicants should, among other efforts, identify the need for funding, their approach to using the funds, specific activities that are crucial to the success of the program, and desired objectives and benefits

---

[30]42 U.S.C. § 3796dd(b)(1)–(2).

[31]Domestic Working Group, Grant Accountability Project, *Guide to Opportunities for Improving Grant Accountability* (Washington, D.C.: October 2005).

[32]Although the Domestic Working Group Guide provides numerous recommendations for overall grant management, we focused our review on those criteria most pertinent to the design of grant applications.

GAO-13-521 Community Policing Hiring Grants

anticipated—and then logically connect these efforts to a plan for measuring results.

We found through our analysis of a systematic random sample of 103 CHP-funded applications for fiscal years 2010, 2011, and 2012 that the application could be enhanced by applying these best practices to clarify for applicants that CHP-funded officers are required to be the personnel specifically engaged in the community policing activities described on the application. According to our analysis of the application sample, we estimate that less than 20 percent of the applications funded in these years contained evidence showing how additional officers would be deployed in support of community policing. [33]

Several of the questions in the 2010, 2011, and 2012 applications ask for information on the agency-wide actions grantees plan to undertake to facilitate community policing. COPS Office officials reported that individual CHP-funded officers are expected to implement the items indicated in the implementation plan. These actions could include implementing recruitment and hiring practices that reflect an orientation toward problem solving and community engagement, enhancing information technology systems, and implementing organizational performance measurement systems that include community policing metrics. COPS Office officials agreed that the application could be clearer by stating the requirement that CHP-funded officers should be the ones who are specifically engaged in CHP-funded activities.

Revising the application to clarify for applicants that CHP-funded officers are required to be the personnel specifically engaged in the community policing activities described on the application, consistent with best practices, would better position the COPS office to ascertain from applicants how these particular officers' activities would advance community policing.

---

[33] The point estimate is 17 percent, and the associated 95 percent confidence interval is (10, 25).

The COPS Office's Monitoring Process Assesses How Grantees Are Using CHP Funds to Advance Community Policing, but Could Be Improved through Additional Monitoring Guidance

The COPS Office Takes a Risk-Based Approach to Grant Monitoring and Has Processes to Monitor How Grantees Are Using Funds

To help ensure that grantees are implementing the activities and meeting the financial requirements they committed to in their respective applications, the COPS Office is required to monitor at least 10 percent of its open, active grant funding annually.[34] According to the Domestic Working Group's guide for improving grant accountability, it is important that agencies identify, prioritize, and manage potential at-risk grantees. Consistent with this best practice and to fulfill its statutory monitoring requirement, the COPS Office uses a risk-based approach to select which grantees to monitor and visit using its Grant Assessment Tool (GAT), which is currently used by the COPS Office to assess grantee risk.[35] The GAT uses criteria to generate individual risk scores, as illustrated in table 3, and a final, comprehensive risk assessment score is computed for grantees.

---

[34]See 42 U.S.C. § 3712h.

[35]According to COPS Office officials, all grantees are required to submit quarterly progress reports that provide financial and programmatic information, such as their progress in implementing the community policing plans they described in their grant applications.

Table 3: Community Oriented Policing (COPS) Office Grant Risk Assessment Tool Criteria Examples

Risk criteria	Risk score
Grant award value	More than $1,000,000: 4 More than $500,000: 2 Less than $500,000: 0
Late grant federal financial reports: These reports are submitted quarterly and are used to report the amount of federal grant and local matching funds used to implement the grant.	More than two late reports: 2 One late report: 1 No late reports: 0
Waiver on matching funds requirement authorized	Received a waiver: 4 Did not receive a waiver: 0
Local matching funds required	Yes: 2 No: 0
Undergoing a DOJ (IG) audit or grantee has recent open audit recommendations: The IG conducts performance and financial audits of select individual grantees, and these audits can include recommendations related to these grantees.	Yes: 4 No: 0
Grant modifications requested by grantees: Modifications can involve but are not limited to cost items or the classification of the hiring, such as changing awards from new hire to rehire.	2 modifications requested: 1 3 modifications requested: 3
Grant extensions: Grantees can request extensions on grant time periods in order to implement their grants.	Extension provided for between 2 and 5 years: 2 Extension provided for more than 5 years: 4

Source: GAO analysis of the COPS Office's risk assessment approach.

Once the monitors review what the GAT has generated, they are to develop a plan for monitoring those grantees with the highest risk scores. According to the COPS Office's monitoring standards—a guide that describes the responsibilities of grant monitors—the COPS Office monitors these grantees in a number of ways, including, but not limited to, on-site monitoring, office-based grant reviews, and complaint and legal reviews.[36] During on-site monitoring visits, monitors are required by the monitoring standards to review and compare the proposed projects and activities contained in grant applications and quarterly progress and financial status reports with those of the grantees' performance and progress in carrying them out.[37] Upon completion of their visits, monitors

---

[36]DOJ, *Grant Monitoring Standards and Guidelines for Hiring and Redeployment, Community Oriented Policing Services (COPS) Office,* (Washington, D.C.: Sept.16, 2004).

[37]In some cases, OJP's Office of the Chief Financial Officer will conduct joint site visits with COPS Office programmatic monitors in cases requiring more in-depth reviews of grantee financial management of grant funding.

are required to document their observations and assessments in a grant-monitoring report and cite any grant compliance issues, which may be cited in categories including community policing, retention, allowable costs, and the source and amount of matching funds.

Office-based grant reviews, which are used to provide detailed monitoring for those grantees that are not selected for on-site monitoring using the GAT, are similar to on-site reviews in that monitors are required to review grantee documentation, including the application, and follow up directly with the grantee to collect any additional information and documentation on how grantees are using funds. This type of monitoring, according to COPS Office monitoring standards, allows the COPS Office to monitor a larger number of grantees than would be possible through on-site monitoring alone. In addition to these monitoring methods, the COPS Office also uses complaint reviews to investigate internal and external complaints, such as those raised by the media and citizens, regarding grantee noncompliance. The COPS Office's Legal Division also conducts additional monitoring related to, among other things, supplanting—using federal funds to replace state or local funds—and DOJ IG investigations of grantees involving fraud. According to the monitoring standards, all of these monitoring efforts help the COPS Office determine whether the grantees are complying with the requirements of the grant and that funds are spent properly. Accordingly, the COPS Office uses these various monitoring methods to identify any grant violations, such as not using the funds to hire officers for deployment in community policing, and recommend resolutions to these violations. In cases where the grantee has failed to remedy violations identified by the monitor, the grantee, according to the monitoring standards, may be faced with adverse current and future determinations regarding its suitability for receiving grant funds, the suspension or termination of grant funds, repayment of expended grant funds to the COPS Office, and even criminal liability in the event of fraud.

The COPS Office Has Standards for Monitoring Supplanting, but Could Strengthen Its Guidance for Documenting Supplanting Analysis in Monitoring Reports

The authorizing statute for the COPS grant programs, including CHP, requires that grantees not supplant state and local funding, but rather use the federal funds for activities beyond what would have been available without a grant.[38] As a condition of accepting COPS Office funding, grant applicants must certify they will use grant funding only to increase the total amount of funds available for the hiring or rehiring of law enforcement officers and not supplant state and local funding. To identify supplanting risks, the COPS Office developed standards for monitors to use in assessing the potential for supplanting, which is one of the compliance issues monitors are required to evaluate. Monitors can use these supplanting standards in all forms of monitoring, including on-site, office-based desk, complaint, and Legal Division reviews. The standards contain clear guidance for identifying potential noncompliance with supplanting standards. For example, according to the COPS Office's grant monitoring standards and, as illustrated in table 4, there are four major patterns of risk associated with supplanting.[39]

---

[38]42 U.S.C. § 3796dd-3. For the purpose of COPS Office grants, supplanting means using COPS Office grant funds to replace state or local funding—or, in the case of Indian tribal governments, funding supplied by the Bureau of Indian Affairs—that otherwise would have been spent on the specific law enforcement purpose of the COPS Office grant award.

[39]DOJ, Office of Community Oriented Policing Services, *Grant Monitoring Standards and Guidelines for Hiring and Redeployment*, (Washington, D.C.: Sept. 16, 2004).

Table 4: Community Oriented Policing (COPS) Office Supplanting Identification Guidance for Monitors

Supplanting risk pattern	Description
Hiring sworn officers before the grant award date	This may be an indication that the grantee is using COPS Hiring Program (CHP) funding to support officers already onboard which is inconsistent with the program requirements to increase the total number of officers.
Delays in filling vacant locally funded sworn officer positions	Any delay in filling locally funded vacancies must not be a direct result of receiving grant funds; otherwise, it may be considered supplanting.
Decreases in the baseline level of funding for locally funded sworn officers during the grant period	For any reductions in state and local funding levels for sworn officers that occurred in proximity to receiving the CHP award, the grantee must show that such reductions were unassociated with the award by providing evidence, such as city council minutes, memorandums, budgets, or other documentation, that shows the decreases were unassociated with receiving a CHP award.
Decreases in the baseline level of sworn officer positions during the grant period	If, during the grant period, the state and local baseline levels for the number of sworn officers has decreased, the grantee must be able to demonstrate by providing evidence, such as city council minutes, memorandums, budgets, or other documentation, that shows the decreases during the grant period were unassociated with CHP funding. Such documentation could show decreases related to fiscal distress, civilianization of sworn positions, or a management reorganization unrelated to the CHP award, to comply with the nonsupplanting requirement.[a]

Source: GAO analysis of COPS Office policy.

[a]Some law enforcement agencies employ civilian police employees to conduct criminal justice work, such as crime identification and analysis. Civilianization of sworn positions refers to the use of civilian employees instead of sworn police officers to conduct criminal justice work.

The CHP supplanting standards also require grant monitors to conduct an analysis and review of supporting evidence to ensure grantees have not engaged in supplanting. Some of the acceptable documentation, according to the COPS Office, can be:

- budget documents that can show the replacement rate of officers has remained consistent,
- documentation that shows the grantee has experienced fiscal distress, or
- city council minutes showing there has been difficulty in local hiring.

The standards do not specify how monitors should document their analysis and conclusions about potential supplanting issues in the monitoring reports they prepare after site visits. According to COPS Office officials, these reports are a critical component of the monitoring process The COPS Monitoring Operations Manual—a technical guide for monitoring—requires monitors to identify and provide relevant details in monitoring reports where supplanting is identified. However, it does not require monitors to document their analysis and conclusions in instances in which the determination is ultimately made that supplanting has not occurred. As a result, it may be unclear how the monitors assessed these cases to reach conclusions that supplanting had not occurred in these instances. In our review of the monitoring reports for 39 of 55 grantees that had already begun to use CHP funds and were visited by grant monitors, we found 21 grantees for which there was a pattern of risk for potential supplanting. For 16 of these 21, we concluded that the site visit reports clearly documented the analysis and conclusions reached by the monitors regarding supplanting issues. For example, one monitor noted in a site visit report that potential supplanting existed because a police department failed to fill local vacancies at the same time it hired officers using COPS grant funds. The monitor determined that there was no violation for supplanting based on information provided during and after the site visit demonstrating that the department was taking active and timely steps to fill local vacancies and that the department was prohibited from filling vacancies earlier because of a town-wide spending freeze. The site visit report listed the documentation that the monitor reviewed in making a determination that there was no violation, including copies of budget documents demonstrating town-wide cuts in personnel and the town's fiscal distress, a memorandum implementing a town-wide spending freeze, an online job posting for the vacant officer positions, and the police department's request to the town for authorization to fill the vacancies.

However, for the remaining 5 of 21 grantees, we found that the monitors did not document their assessments of supplanting issues, and it was not clear how they reached conclusions regarding potential supplanting. The reports for these 5 grantees indicated that there were delays in filling vacancies for locally funded officer positions at the time when officers were hired for CHP-funded positions. For example, in one report, the data showed that there were over 50 vacant locally funded positions in fiscal year 2010 that continued to be unfilled in fiscal year 2011, when the same department hired 27 officers with COPS funding. When the monitor visited the department in August 2012, there were still 59 locally funded vacancies. The site visit report noted that the department anticipated filling the vacancies in November 2012 and did not discuss any supplanting compliance issues. The report did not provide details on documentation reviewed or other information obtained to demonstrate the analysis performed or the basis for determinations on potential supplanting issues. It was unclear from this whether or how the monitor had assessed potential supplanting issues. In following up with the COPS

Office on this case, officials provided us with additional evidence that the monitor had assessed supplanting and determined it had not occurred. Specifically, the monitor obtained documentation from the police department supporting that the department had completed recruitment for the positions and was in the middle of the applicant selection process. COPS Office officials also provided us with additional information that monitors had obtained on site visits for the other 4 cases that was not included in the monitoring reports, but supported that the monitors had assessed potential supplanting issues and determined supplanting had not occurred. Including this information in the site visit reports would document that supplanting issues were properly assessed in accordance with the monitoring standards.

Given the statutory prohibition against the supplanting of federal funds and the importance of documentation for agency accountability, monitors should consistently document the results of their supplanting analysis in the monitoring reports for on-site monitoring. According to Standards for Internal Control in the Federal Government, the documentation of agency activities is a key element of accountability for decisions.[40] By enhancing the COPS Office's monitoring guidance, such as its standards or operations manual, to require monitors to document the results of their supplanting analysis in the on-site monitoring reports for instances where the determination is made that no supplanting has occurred, the COPS Office could be better positioned to ensure that monitors are consistently assessing supplanting and that CHP funding is supplementing and not replacing state and local funding. Additionally, ensuring that monitors consistently document the results of their supplanting analysis would increase transparency and enhance oversight of CHP funds.

Conclusions

The COPS Office awarded approximately $1.7 billion in grant funds from fiscal year 2008 through 2012 for hiring officers to advance community policing. To ensure that grantees are using the funds as intended by the program, the COPS Office's CHP application collects information required by statute, including information on how applicants will implement community policing on an agency-wide scale. However, the application does not require prospective grantees to provide information on the specific community policing activities of CHP-funded officers or a

---

[40]GAO/AIMD-00-21.3.1/.

commensurate number of experienced locally funded officers. Revising the application to clarify for applicants that CHP-funded officers are required to be the personnel specifically engaged in the community policing activities described on the application, consistent with best practices, would better position the COPS office to ascertain from applicants how these particular officers' activities would advance community policing. In addition, we found that while the COPS Office has developed standards and an operations manual for monitors to use in assessing the potential for supplanting, the COPS Office's monitoring standards and operations manual do not require monitors to document their analysis and conclusions in instances in which the determination is ultimately made that supplanting has not occurred. We found that for 5 of the 21 grantees for whom we identified as at risk for supplanting, the monitors included information in the monitoring reports on supplanting, but did not document their assessments of the supplanting issues. Enhancing the COPS Office's monitoring guidance, such as its standards or operations manual, to require monitors to document the results of their supplanting analysis in the on-site monitoring reports for instances where the determination is made that no supplanting has occurred could better position the COPS Office to ensure that monitors are consistently assessing supplanting and ensuring that CHP funding is supplementing and not replacing state and local funding.

Recommendations for Executive Action

To further enhance the accountability of the CHP, the Attorney General should direct the COPS Office Director to take the following two actions:

1. revise the CHP application to clarify for applicants that CHP-funded officers are required to be the personnel specifically engaged in the community policing activities described on the application; and

2. enhance the COPS Office's guidance, such as its monitoring standards or operations manual, by requiring monitors to document the results of their supplanting analysis in on-site monitoring reports for instances where the determination is made that no supplanting has occurred.

Agency Comments and Our Evaluation

We provided a draft of this report to DOJ and the COPS Office for review and comment. The COPS Office provided written comments on the draft report, which are summarized below and reproduced in full in appendix III. The COPS Office concurred with the two recommendations in the report and identified actions planned to implement the recommendations. The COPS Office also discussed concerns it had with the discussion of the grant application and wording of the second recommendation in the draft report.

The COPS Office concurred with the first recommendation, that the COPS Office revise the CHP application to clarify for applicants that CHP-funded officers are required to be the personnel specifically engaged in the community policing activities described on the application. The COPS Office stated that, in response to the recommendation, it clarified in the current *CHP Grant Owner's Manual* and will clarify in subsequent years' CHP applications that the questions in the grant application apply not only to the agency overall but to the CHP-funded officers as well. Once the COPS Office has taken action to fully implement this recommendation, it will be better positioned to ascertain from applicants that officers' activities would advance community policing.

While the COPS Office concurred with the recommendation, it raised concerns in its letter about how we characterized the way the COPS Office collects information via the CHP application on the activities of CHP-funded officers. Specifically, the COPS Office disagreed with the statements that (1) the 2012 CHP application does not specifically ask applicants to explain how CHP-funded officers will be deployed in community policing and that (2) less than 20 percent of the applications funded in 2010, 2011, and 2012 contained evidence showing how additional CHP-funded officers would be deployed to community policing. According to the COPS Office, the CHP application contains over 70 individual close-ended questions and 3 narrative questions regarding activities that CHP-funded officers and agencies will commit to as a requirement of the grant. The report acknowledges that the COPS Office collects an array of information from applicants on the agency-wide activities they plan to conduct. However, our analysis—including the analysis of a systematic random sample of CHP-funded applications—was intended to demonstrate the extent to which CHP applications contained information about how additional officers would be deployed in community policing in the absence of the application not specifically asking applicants to describe which community policing activities individual CHP-funded officers will undertake. Revising the application to clarify for applicants that CHP-funded officers are required to be the personnel specifically engaged in the community policing activities described on the application, consistent with best practices, would better position the COPS Office to ascertain from applicants how these particular officers' activities would advance community policing.

The COPS Office also disagreed with a statement in the draft report that the COPS Office stated that there could be benefits to revising the application to more clearly delineate the activities in which CHP-funded officers should be engaged. Rather, the COPS Office stated in its letter that the application could be clearer by stating that the office is requiring that COPS-funded officers should be the ones who are specifically engaged in CHP- funded activities. We modified the recommendation and related language in the report to reflect this point. We provided the modified recommendation language to the COPS office, and on September 19th in an e-mail from CHP program officials, the office concurred.

The COPS Office concurred with the second recommendation to enhance the COPS Office's monitoring guidance by requiring monitors to document the results of their supplanting analysis in on-site monitoring reports for instances where the determination is made that no supplanting has occurred. The office stated that it had checks and balances in its monitoring practices on the review of grantee documents and guidance for documenting analysis results when supplanting is identified.

While the COPS Office concurred with the recommendation, it noted in its letter that our recommendation as originally worded implied that the existing monitoring guidance does not require grant monitors to document the results of their supplanting analysis for cases in which supplanting has been identified. Since the COPS Monitoring Operations Manual requires monitors to identify and provide relevant details in the monitoring reports regarding instances in which supplanting has occurred, the COPS Office requested that we amend the recommendation with language stating that the monitoring reports be enhanced by ensuring that monitors document the results of their supplanting analysis in instances that do not give rise to supplanting concerns. We adjusted the recommendation and related language accordingly to clarify this point.

Further, in response to the recommendation, the COPS Office outlined initiatives it has implemented to modify its COPS Monitoring Operations Manual that reflect changes to data collection tools and instructions on how monitors should document their supplanting analysis, including instances in which monitors determine that no supplanting has occurred, in the monitoring reports. These actions, if implemented effectively, should address the intent of the recommendation.

We are sending copies of this report to the Assistant Attorney General For Administration, and interested congressional committees. In addition,

this report is available at no charge on the GAO website at
http://www.gao.gov.

If you or your staff have any questions about this report, please contact
me at (202) 512-9627 or maurerd@gao.gov. Contact points for our
Offices of Congressional Relations and Public Affairs may be found on
the last page of this report. Key contributors to this report are listed in
appendix III.

David C. Maurer
Director
Homeland Security and Justice Issues

Appendix I: Objectives, Scope, and Methodology

This report answers the following questions: (1) From fiscal years 2008 through 2012, in what areas of the country was the Community Oriented Policing Services (COPS) Hiring Program (CHP) funding disbursed and to what extent did award amounts vary during this period? (2) To what extent does the COPS Office's grant application collect information about how applicants plan to use CHP-funded officers to advance community policing? (3) To what extent does the COPS Office's monitoring process assess whether grantees are using funds to advance community policing?

To address the first question, we reviewed the history of the COPS Office's programs and related award data from the most recent 5 fiscal years—2008 through 2012—and confirmed that CHP received the largest share of award funds as compared with other programs administered by the COPS Office during this period. We also analyzed COPS Office documentation, such as *Grant Owner's Manuals* and COPS Office website materials, to learn about each COPS program's origin and emphasis. To determine which areas of the United States have received CHP funding, we analyzed the allocation of CHP grant awards—and the numbers of officers funded—by state and mapped the CHP grant award data. Additionally, we analyzed CHP award lists for fiscal years 2008 through 2012 to determine the average CHP entry-level officer salary and benefits by state, and assessed them for variation.[1] To assess the reliability of data used in our review, we reviewed system tests that the COPS Office conducts periodically to ensure data reliability and interviewed COPS Office officials about the integrity of the data they provided to us. We determined that the data were sufficiently reliable for the purposes of our report. We also interviewed COPS Office officials responsible for managing the CHP program to verify grant program information, determine factors that could account for variations in grant award amounts, and learn about other administrative aspects of the program.

To address the second question, we assessed CHP documentation, including CHP grant applications and *Grant Owner's Manuals* to determine how the COPS Office's application collects information about

---

[1]We focused our review of grant award lists from fiscal years 2009 through 2011 because during this period the COPS Office awarded each grantee the full amount it cost the grantee to pay the salaries and benefits of each funded officer. In both fiscal years 2008 and 2012, appropriations language removed the caps, as we discuss later in the report.

how applicants plan to use CHP-funded officers to advance community
policing. We examined the CHP authorizing statute and best practices for
grants management identified in the Domestic Working Group Grant
Accountability Project's Guide to Opportunities for Improving Grant
Accountability and compared the criteria outlining promising practices for
grant applications, such as designing applications to gather sufficient
information for making award decisions, with the COPS Office's
approaches for designing the CHP application.[2]

To better understand these approaches, we reviewed the CHP
application design, allowable activities, and the COPS Office's criteria for
selecting awardees. Specifically, we used elements of the CHP
authorizing statute and key best practices for grant management to
develop a data collection instrument we used to review all applications
from a sample of 103 out of the 841 grants awarded during fiscal years
2010, 2011, and 2012. We chose to evaluate applications from these 3
fiscal years to provide an assessment of the most recent fiscal years'
application design. Using the data collection instrument, we reviewed the
application sample to determine, among other items, the applications'
level of detail in describing applicants' planned use of funds. Each
application was first reviewed by an analyst, and the information recorded
in each completed instrument was then verified by a second analyst. To
ensure a selection of grants representative of the dollar amount
distribution in the population of 841 awarded grants, we sorted the
population by the grant dollar amount and then selected a systematic
random sample of 104 grants.[3] During our review, we discovered that 1
grant in our sample was out of scope because the grantee did not accept
the grant funds and was no longer considered an active grantee. We
reviewed the remaining 103 grant applications in our sample and treated
them as a simple random sample for purposes of estimation. Because we
followed a probability procedure based on random selections, our sample
is only one of a large number of samples that we might have drawn.
Since each sample could have provided different estimates, we express
our confidence in the precision of our particular sample's results as a 95

[2]Domestic Working Group, Grant Accountability Project, Guide to Opportunities for
Improving Grant Accountability (Washington, D.C.: October 2005).

[3]A systematic random sample is a method of sample selection in which the population is
listed in some order, in this instance dollar amount of grant awarded, and every kth
element is selected randomly for the sample.

GAO-13-521 Community Policing Hiring Grants

percent confidence interval (e.g., plus or minus 9 percentage points). This is the interval that would contain the actual population value for 95 percent of the samples we could have drawn. With the finite population correction factor, the precision for estimates drawn from this sample is no greater than plus or minus 9 percentage points at the 95 percent level of confidence. To ensure the reliability of data used in our review, we interviewed COPS Office officials about the integrity of the data they provided to us and reviewed system tests that the COPS Office conducts periodically to ensure data reliability. We also ensured that the electronic data CHP applicants submitted could not be altered once submitted to the COPS Office. We determined that the data were sufficiently reliable for the purposes of our report.

We also conducted interviews with a nonprobability sample of 20 CHP grantees in California, Florida, Illinois, Massachusetts, Texas, and Wisconsin. We selected these grantees from five metropolitan areas according to criteria that included the amount of funding received by the grantees, the concentration of grantees within a metropolitan area to maximize the amount of information we could collect, and the population size served by grantees. The results of these interviews are not generalizable to all grantees, but provided insight, among other things, into how CHP grant funds are used locally to advance community policing. Finally, we interviewed COPS Office officials who oversee the application process to gather further information on the design of the application, including how the applications were scored.

To address the third question, we obtained and examined the monitoring reports for 55 grantees awarded CHP grants from the 3 most recent fiscal years—2010 through 2012—with completed, available monitoring reports.[4] The COPS Office produced these reports following the on-site monitoring visits it conducts with grantees to assess their progress and identify any compliance issues for CHP grants. Specifically, we developed a data collection instrument to review the monitoring reports to assess the extent to which the COPS Office identified and documented supplanting. We used the questions on the data collection instrument to make these assessments. Each report was first reviewed by an analyst, and the

---

[4]As with the grant applications we selected for review, we selected these 3 years because they reflected the most recent active CHP awards, each of which remains open for a 3-year grant term. These 55 grantees were all of the grantees from this period for which the COPS Office had completed CHP grant-monitoring reports at the time we began our audit.

information recorded in each completed instrument was then verified by a
second analyst. We then compared the COPS Office's monitoring
practices with best practices identified in the Domestic Working Group
Grant Accountability Project's Guide to Opportunities for Improving Grant
Accountability; Standards for Internal Control in the Federal Government;
and COPS Office guidance, such as its grant-monitoring standards.[5] For
context, we also considered findings from prior GAO work on program
evaluation and the COPS Office's management of its grant programs.[6] To
understand how the COPS Office assesses the potential for supplanting,
we used COPS Office guidance on determining supplanting in reviewing
the monitoring reports to identify grantees at risk of using CHP funds to
replace state and local funds. Additionally, we assessed how the monitors
addressed and documented instances in which grantees were vulnerable
to supplanting, such as collecting and evaluating additional budget
documentation from grantees. During the site visits, we interviewed CHP
grantees about, among other topics, the community policing strategies
they employed with CHP funding and whether their agencies had
increased the number of officers dedicated to community policing relative
to the number of officers hired with CHP funding. We also interviewed
COPS Office officials who oversee the monitoring process about their
monitoring practices and discussed with officials how monitoring provided
relevant context to what grantees and the COPS Office considered
progress. We also obtained the perspective of the COPS Office on the
performance of its grant monitors in identifying and documenting
instances of potential supplanting in the reports for on-site monitoring

We conducted this performance audit from August 2012 to September
2013 in accordance with generally accepted government auditing
standards. Those standards require that we plan and perform the audit to
obtain sufficient, appropriate evidence to provide a reasonable basis for
our findings and conclusions based on our audit objectives. We believe

---

[5]Domestic Working Group, Grant Accountability Project, *Guide to Opportunities for
Improving Grant Accountability.*

[6]GAO, *Designing Evaluations: 2012 Revision,* GAO-12-208G (Washington D.C.: Jan. 31,
2012). DOJ Office of the Inspector General, *Improving the Office of Community Oriented
Policing Services' Grant Awarding, Monitoring, and Program Evaluation Processes,*
(Washington, D.C.: June, 2009). DOJ, *Grant Monitoring Standards and Guidelines for
Hiring and Redeployment,* Community Oriented Policing Services (COPS) Office,
(Washington, D.C.: Sept.16, 2004).

that the evidence obtained provides a reasonable basis for our findings
and conclusions based on our audit objectives.

Appendix II: How Proactive and Reactive Policing Differ

This appendix corresponds with figure 1 in the report, which is an interactive figure. Table 5 contains the text that is not accessible to readers of print copies of this report.

Table 5: How Proactive and Reactive Policing Differ

Aspects of proactive and reactive policing	Description in pop-up box
Reactive policing	
911	Citizens report crime by dialing 911 and in some jurisdictions, can text police departments to report crime.
Police response	Generally, police assigned to the police patrol answer 911 service calls based upon their geographical area of assignment.
Reactive policing Intervention	Sworn police officers responding to 911 service calls generally have a variety of options to address a specific crime, such as issue warnings and citations or arrest suspects of crime for referral to the court system.
Proactive policing	
Crime problem identification	Identified through strategies such as Community Policing—through proactive interaction with the community, officers receive information about specific types of crime problems. Through this proactive interaction, officers gain legitimacy with the community, which creates a self-perpetuating cycle of community feedback.
	Examples of Proactive Community Policing Activities:
	Neighborhood Police Liaisons
	Police communicate with citizens in an assigned neighborhood and engage in order maintenance, such as ordinance violations and housing code enforcement, which can lead to crime.
	School Resource Officers
	Deployed inside schools to proactively address such problems as drug use and distribution, and to generally prevent delinquency.
Intelligence gathering	Gathered through a variety of police strategies such as
	police investigations in response to reported crime,
	911 service call reporting,
	cooperative victims assisting police, and
	specialized units gathering intelligence such as anti-gang or neighborhood response.
Crime analysis	Software programs such as CompStat allow law enforcement to collect and analyze data in order to map areas of high crime.
	Some police departments employ crime analysts who are typically non-sworn employees to conduct analysis to identify causes of crime problems so that departments can dedicate an appropriate level of resources to intervention strategies.

Aspects of proactive and reactive policing	Description in pop-up box
Proactive policing intervention	Through the identification and analysis of crime information, law enforcement personnel use a variety of strategies to prevent and solve crime problems, including:
	Order maintenance
	Whereby disorder in the community such as graffiti and abandoned cars can be addressed and therefore reduces the chances that particular areas will experience more serious crime in the future.
	Hot spot policing
	Through the use of crime mapping, law enforcement can prevent crime through the redeployment of officers to areas experiencing high levels of crime. Officers can be deployed in a variety of ways, including bike, automobile, and foot patrol, where they may be able to respond to 911 service calls quickly or may generally be seen as a crime deterrence.
	Multiagency task forces
	Some law enforcement agencies leverage resources across law enforcement agencies using analyzed data such as data about human or illegal drug trafficking to interdict these crimes.
Resolution	Not all interventions require crime problems and the perpetrators of crime to be addressed by the court system. Interventions such as order maintenance are known to deter future crime and generally do not require arrest and referral of cases to the court system.
	Other results that are more likely to require the referral of cases to the court system are when the interventions are directly focused on perpetrators of crime and not necessarily on the environmental conditions related to crime. Such referrals and successful adjudications both remove criminals from society and provide for a general deterrence of crime.

Source: GAO.

Appendix III: Comments from the Department of Justice

U.S. DEPARTMENT OF JUSTICE
OFFICE OF COMMUNITY ORIENTED POLICING SERVICES

COPS

Office of the Director
145 N Street, N.E., Washington, DC 20530

August 30, 2013

Mr. David C. Maurer
Director
Homeland Security and Justice Issues
Government Accountability Office
441 G Street, NW
Washington, DC 20548

Dear Mr. Maurer:

Thank you for the opportunity to review and comment on the draft Government Accountability Office (GAO) report entitled, "Community Policing Hiring Grants: Grant Application and Monitoring Processes Could Be Improved to Further Ensure Grantees Advance Community Policing" (GAO-13-521). The Department of Justice (DOJ) Office of Community Oriented Policing Services (COPS) appreciates the work of the GAO and has carefully considered the findings and recommendations presented in GAO's draft report.

The COPS Office thanks the GAO for its review of the COPS Office's grant management funding and oversight practices of our community policing grants from 2008 to 2012. We believe that we have followed all statutory requirements and have made awards to grantees in a fair and impartial manner based on those requirements. We are pleased that, despite its extensive review, the GAO found no evidence to the contrary and that variation in awards across states can be explained due to statutory factors and regional differences. We are also pleased that the GAO did not identify any instances of grantee supplanting; instead, COPS grants are providing agencies' funding for additional sworn officer positions that they would otherwise not be able to fund with State or local funds.

While we acknowledge the GAO's comprehensive examination of the COPS Office's application and monitoring processes and practices, we would like to address a few points which need to be clarified with regard to community policing questions.

Community Policing Questions on Applications

In the Highlights and on page 19, the draft report states that "… less than 20 percent of the applications funded in 2010, 2011, and 2012 contained evidence showing how additional officers would be deployed to support community policing." Further, the report states on page 19 that the 2012 CHP application does not specifically ask applicants to explain how CHP-funded officers will be deployed into community policing. It states, as an example, that the application does not ask applicants to provide information on what community policing activities CHP-funded officers will be undertaking (such as attending community meetings).

ADVANCING PUBLIC SAFETY THROUGH COMMUNITY POLICING

Mr. David C. Maurer
August 30, 2013
Page 2

The COPS Office disagrees with these statements as 100 percent of COPS Office applicants
provide information on the activities that additional officers (or like number of veteran officers)
will be engaged in as a part of their required activities. Specifically, the Community Policing
section of the CHP application collects a vast amount of information from grantees regarding
their planned community policing activities. In addition to their community policing plan, the
application also collects information from over 60 specific questions regarding agencies' current
community policing activities, and their current fiscal health and crime situation that are used to
evaluate their applications.

The community policing plan contains over 70 individual close-ended questions and three
narrative questions regarding activities that these officers and agencies will commit to as a
requirement of their grant. The application collects information on a variety of commonly
accepted community policing activities that these officers, or a like number of veteran officers,
will be involved in including: the specific problems they seek to address with this grant funding;
the proposed approach to addressing the identified problems; the primary goal in addressing the
identified problems; the specific information they are going to analyze to better understand the
problem; the number and names of specific partners that they are going to work with; the steps
they are going to take to formalize these partnerships; the specific data that they are going to
examine to evaluate the quality of their response; the specific public safety outcomes that they
hope to achieve; and the specific broad organizational changes that they are going to engage in as
a result of receiving grant funding. It should also be noted that these 70 activities are
individually tracked as a part of agencies' quarterly progress reporting requirements. For a
variety of reasons, we are confident that collecting a mix of close-ended and narrative questions
regarding agencies' community policing plans is highly preferable to collecting only narrative
statements resulting in all applicants providing detailed information on the community policing
activities the grant-funded officers will perform, if the agency is awarded a CHP grant.

In the Highlights and on page 19, the draft report further states that "COPS Office officials stated
that revising the application to more clearly delineate the activities CHP-funded officers should
be engaged in as part of the implementation plan could be beneficial." This does not accurately
portray what we stated, as we believe that the application does clearly delineate the activities that
the CHP-funded officers (or like number of veteran officers) should be engaged in. Rather, our
statement was that we agreed that the application could be clearer in that we are requiring that
these specific COPS-funded officers (or a like number of veteran officers) should be the ones
who are specifically engaged in these activities, not that the activities themselves require greater
clarification. To this point, we have already revised the current grant owner's manual to further
emphasize this point and will be revising our application materials for future years to clarify this
for applicants. We appreciate the GAO bringing this point of clarification to our attention.

Responses to Specific GAO Recommendations

The draft GAO report contains two Recommendations for Executive Action to the COPS Office,
which are restated in bold text below and are followed by our response.

Mr. David C. Maurer
August 30, 2013
Page 3

1. **Revise the CHP application to ask applicants to provide additional information describing the specific community policing activities of those officers to be hired or rehired with CHP grant funds or of a commensurate number of experienced locally funded officers deployed in support of community policing.**

The COPS Office agrees with the Recommendation for Executive Action. As explained earlier, the CHP application includes a comprehensive set of close-ended and narrative questions that captures information on the specific community policing activities that the grant-funded officers (or like number of veteran officers) will perform if the applicant is awarded a grant. However, to address the GAO's concerns, in subsequent CHP applications, the COPS Office will clarify that the questions in the section specifically apply to the grant-funded officers, or an equal number of veteran officers, that the grantee deploys to perform the community policing activities during the grant period and not only to the grantee agency overall.

2. **Enhance the COPS Office's monitoring standards by requiring monitors to document the results of their supplanting analysis in the monitoring reports for on-site monitoring.**

The COPS Office agrees with the Recommendation for Executive Action. The COPS Office is committed to ensuring grantee compliance with the non-supplanting requirement and provides extensive guidance on the requirement and how to comply with it in our grant documents. The COPS Office has also incorporated checks and balances in its monitoring practices on the review of grantee documents and practices to ensure grantees are following the non-supplanting requirement. In addition, nonsupplanting protocols are captured in the COPS Monitoring Operations Manual (MOM).

The COPS Office Grant Monitoring Division's (GMD) monitoring standards currently require Grant Monitoring Specialists to obtain documentation on all identified supplanting analyses and to document identified supplanting issues in the site visit report for appropriate follow-up by Grant Monitoring Specialists. To address the GAO's concerns, the COPS Office has implemented the following initiatives to ensure that the site visit report also includes the Grant Monitoring Specialist's supplanting analysis for instances that do not result in a supplanting concern:

- Revised data collection tools to include the hiring and non-hiring grant checklists by including clearer instructions on how monitors should document compliance analysis.
- Revised the site visit reports to include moving the compliance sections to each grant checklist in addition to providing clearer language on how to document compliance analysis.
- Included a receipt of grantee documentation checklist into the monitoring processes.
- The Monitoring Operations Manual will be revised to include all of the documents and revisions listed above.

Mr. David C. Maurer
August 30, 2013
Page 4

Based upon the aforementioned, the COPS Office respectfully requests that the GAO
recommendation be amended. The current GAO recommendation implies that the existing
monitoring standards do not require grant monitors to document the results of their supplanting
analysis, which is not accurate. The GAO report is narrowly focused on those instances when a
grant monitor does not document the results of his/her supplanting analysis in the monitoring
report when a determination is made that no supplanting has occurred. Therefore, COPS
suggests that the recommendation read as follows:

*"Enhance the COPS Office's on-site monitoring reports by ensuring grant monitors document
the results of supplanting analysis that does not give rise to a supplanting concern."*

If I may be of further assistance to you, please do not hesitate to contact me. Your staff may also
contact Martie Viterito, Program Audit Liaison, at 202-514-6244.

Sincerely,

Joshua A. Ederheimer
Acting Director

cc: Rometta Horner, Audit Liaison
     Audit Liaison Group
     Internal Review and Evaluation Office
     Justice Management Division

     Andrea Nicholson, Audit Liaison
     Audit Liaison Group
     Internal Review and Evaluation Office
     Justice Management Division

     Wayne Henry, Acting Deputy Director
     Management Services Directorate
     Office of Community Oriented Policing Services

     Katherine McQuay, Acting Deputy Director
     Community Policing Advancement
     Office of Community Oriented Policing Services

     Sandra Webb, Deputy Director
     Operations Directorate
     Office of Community Oriented Policing Services

Appendix IV: GAO Contact and Staff Acknowledgments

GAO Contact	David C. Maurer, (202) 512-9627 or maurerd@gao.gov
Staff Acknowledgments	In addition to the contact named above, key contributors to this report were Joy Booth, Assistant Director; Glenn Davis, Assistant Director; David Alexander; Carl Barden; Christine Hanson; Eric Hauswirth; Julian King; Linda Miller; Christian Montz; Robin Nye; Brian Schwartz; and Janet Temko.

GAO's Mission	The Government Accountability Office, the audit, evaluation, and investigative arm of Congress, exists to support Congress in meeting its constitutional responsibilities and to help improve the performance and accountability of the federal government for the American people. GAO examines the use of public funds; evaluates federal programs and policies; and provides analyses, recommendations, and other assistance to help Congress make informed oversight, policy, and funding decisions. GAO's commitment to good government is reflected in its core values of accountability, integrity, and reliability.
Obtaining Copies of GAO Reports and Testimony	The fastest and easiest way to obtain copies of GAO documents at no cost is through GAO's website (http://www.gao.gov). Each weekday afternoon, GAO posts on its website newly released reports, testimony, and correspondence. To have GAO e-mail you a list of newly posted products, go to http://www.gao.gov and select "E-mail Updates."
Order by Phone	The price of each GAO publication reflects GAO's actual cost of production and distribution and depends on the number of pages in the publication and whether the publication is printed in color or black and white. Pricing and ordering information is posted on GAO's website, http://www.gao.gov/ordering.htm. Place orders by calling (202) 512-6000, toll free (866) 801-7077, or TDD (202) 512-2537. Orders may be paid for using American Express, Discover Card, MasterCard, Visa, check, or money order. Call for additional information.
Connect with GAO	Connect with GAO on Facebook, Flickr, Twitter, and YouTube. Subscribe to our RSS Feeds or E-mail Updates. Listen to our Podcasts. Visit GAO on the web at www.gao.gov.
To Report Fraud, Waste, and Abuse in Federal Programs	Contact: Website: http://www.gao.gov/fraudnet/fraudnet.htm E-mail: fraudnet@gao.gov Automated answering system: (800) 424-5454 or (202) 512-7470
Congressional Relations	Katherine Siggerud, Managing Director, siggerudk@gao.gov, (202) 512-4400, U.S. Government Accountability Office, 441 G Street NW, Room 7125, Washington, DC 20548
Public Affairs	Chuck Young, Managing Director, youngc1@gao.gov, (202) 512-4800 U.S. Government Accountability Office, 441 G Street NW, Room 7149 Washington, DC 20548

Please Print on Recycled Paper.

www.ingramcontent.com/pod-product-compliance
Lightning Source LLC
Chambersburg PA
CBHW070503290526
45790CB00003B/1077